THE HEALING POWER OF TEA

Writer
Rebecca D. Williams

Contributing Writer
Michele Price Mann

Consultant
Diane L. McKay, Ph.D., F.A.C.N.

Publications International, Ltd.

Cover Photo: Photodisc/Ryan McVay

Writer:
Rebecca D. Williams is a writer specializing in health and medical topics for books, magazines, and newspapers. She enjoys any kind of tea brewed in her grandmother's antique teapot.

Contributing Writer:
Michele Price Mann is a freelance writer from Birmingham, Alabama. Mann has been writing about health and nutrition topics for more than a decade, and she enjoys helping readers make sense of the latest research.

Consultant:
Diane L. McKay, Ph.D., F.A.C.N., is a scientist in the Antioxidants Research Laboratory at the Jean Mayer USDA Human Nutrition Research Center on Aging at Tufts University and an adjunct assistant professor at Tufts University's Friedman School of Nutrition Science and Policy in Boston. She is a member of the American Society for Nutrition and a fellow of the American College of Nutrition.

Table of Contents

A Cupful of Healing

Tea is served with ceremony in Japan, spicy on the streets of Calcutta, with a swirl of milk in London, and sweet as syrup in Charleston. But no matter how you take it, tea is proving to be more than just a soothing and delicious beverage.

Tea has long been considered a healthful drink, and even thousands of years ago it was prescribed for a wide variety of ailments. Now research is revealing the science behind the ancient wisdom. Tea has healing properties that can help prevent diseases as dissimilar as heart disease and cancer.

You'll travel the world in *The Healing Power of Tea*, learning about the hold tea has had on civilization, how tea is grown and processed to produce all those different types and flavors, why and how tea can help prevent an array of diseases, and finally, how to brew the best cup of tea and store your stash.

With *The Healing Power of Tea*, you'll be a tea connoisseur in no time, reaping the healthful rewards of sipping your favorite brew!

Tea's Tantalizing Tale

From imperial beginnings to modern day popularity, tea has had a recurring role in world events. Tea was central to some of the greatest political, social, and economic upheavals in history, and it remains a drink that defines cultures and stirs passions.

Origins in the Orient

Most historians agree that China was the birthplace of tea. Chinese legend attributes the first cup of tea to Emperor Shen Nung, a scientist and herbalist. In about 2737 B.C., the emperor was in his garden boiling water to drink when some leaves from a nearby camellia shrub blew into his cup. He took a drink of the liquid and found it to be flavorful and energizing. Shen Nung was the first to recognize the potential health benefits of tea and is considered the father of Chinese medicine.

Another legend, from India, attributes the discovery of tea to a Buddhist monk named Daruma, or

Bodhidharma, who later became the founder of Zen Buddhism. Daruma went to China as a missionary, and he vowed to meditate day and night without sleeping. He did this for seven years, until he accidentally fell asleep. When he awoke, he was so distraught that he tore off his eyelids so he could never doze again. The legend says the first tea plant grew where his eyelids fell. Tea is considered a gift to monks so they can stay alert during long hours of meditation.

From Medicine to Mainstream

For centuries, tea was mostly a medicinal drink used to treat everything from sore throats to clumsy children. The first documented reference to tea's medicinal use is from a Chinese scholar named Kuo P'o, who in A.D. 350 refers to a "medicinal beverage made by boiling leaves."

Drinking tea became a vital part of Chinese life during the Tang dynasty (A.D. 618 to 906), which is known as the "Golden Age of Tea." During this era, tea became China's national drink, and tea-drinking customs, including tea ceremonies, became an integral part of Chinese culture. One of the most important works in Chinese tea history, the *Ch'a Ching* (*Tea Classic*), was written during this golden age. Still known as one of the quintessential books on tea, the three-volume tome was embraced by the Chinese people, and it elevated tea preparation and tea drinking to an art form.

During the Sung dynasty (A.D. 960 to 1279), tea drinking became a popular social activity. Green tea was the preferred drink, and at first it was prepared by the boiling method. But a new preparation method emerged—tea was powdered and whipped into boiling water to make a frothy drink. The Emperor Hui Tsung (A.D. 1101–1125) was enamored of this kind of tea and even hosted tea contests in his court. Many elements of Japanese tea ceremony rituals have their roots in the preparation methods used in China during this era.

When Genghis Khan and the Mongols overran China, the Sung dynasty collapsed and the tea culture experienced a decline. But in 1368, when the Ming dynasty overthrew the Mongols, tea regained its popularity. Tea growers began experimenting with new ways of processing tea leaves. The leaves were steamed, dried, and crumbled—methods that more closely resemble modern processing methods—and they were steeped in teapots. The loose-leaf tea could be more easily shipped to far-off locations. Tea could now travel the world.

Journey to Japan

There are also two legends about how tea came to Japan. The first tells the story of a Buddhist priest named Yeisei, who on a trip to China noticed that tea drinking kept monks alert during long hours of meditation. Yeisei brought tea back with him to Japan, and he is considered to be the father of tea in that country. Another legend credits a Japanese monk named Dengyo Daishi with bringing the first seeds of the tea shrub to Japan around A.D. 805. However it entered the country, tea quickly became a beloved drink there.

Tea was first used in Zen Buddhist religious ceremonies, and the renowned Japanese tea ceremony was an outgrowth of this practice. The detailed and beautiful ceremony reflects Zen philosophy and inspired the development of many significant Japanese cultural institutions.

Tea Leaves for Europe

For hundreds of years, tea was a secret of the Far East. It wasn't until a Jesuit priest from Portugal ventured to China on a missionary journey in 1560 that a European tasted a cup of tea. Father Jasper de Cruz wrote about the wonders of tea, and word of it quickly spread. The powerful Portuguese navy developed a trade route with China and began importing the leaves to Holland, France, and the Baltic.

After Holland broke political ties with Portugal in 1602, the Dutch began importing tea to their own shores. The Dutch created one of the most successful Asian trading companies, the Dutch East India Company. Because tea was so expensive to import (at one point during the early seventeenth century, it was 100 shillings a pound), at first it was only a rich man's drink. Soon, though, the Dutch began importing a larger supply of tea.

The Dutch were the first to introduce tea to America. The first tea was brought to New Amsterdam

The Etymology of *Tea*

In China and Japan, tea is most often called *ch'a* or *cha,* but in the southeastern Chinese province of Fujian, the Chinese Amoy Dialect for tea, *te,* is pronounced "tay." It was this pronunciation that the Dutch explorers heard when they traveled to China and brought tea to Holland in the early 17th century. They changed the pronunciation to "tea." In other areas of the world, tea is called *chai,* or *shai.*

(later New York) by Peter Stuyvesant, but the drink didn't become popular until English settlers caught wind of the new drink captivating the motherland.

Tea Time for England

England and tea seem as inseparable as America and baseball. But the English weren't all that impressed with tea when it first hit their shores in 1652. It wasn't until King Charles II and his Portuguese bride Catherine de Braganza, both avid tea drinkers, brought the drink to the palace in the latter part of the seventeenth century that tea became popular.

At first only England's nobility and upper classes drank tea; it was too expensive for common folk. As demand increased, however, the British East India Company was granted a virtual monopoly on trade in Asia. This made tea

A Tip for Great Tea

The longtime practice of tipping your waiter or waitress can be traced back to tea. In early English tea gardens, you would typically find a wooden box on the table labeled T.I.P.S., which stood for "to insure prompt service." As you sat down to order, you would put a coin in the T.I.P.S. box to encourage your waiter to deliver your tea promptly—insuring it was hot when it arrived at your table.

more readily available and affordable. By the 1700s, tea was the most popular drink in the British Isles.

As tea's popularity grew, so did places to enjoy it. Coffeehouses and tearooms dotted cities and towns throughout England. But it was the advent and popularity of tea gardens that most transformed British society. Women were first allowed to mingle with men there, and they enjoyed tea, conversations, strolls through beautiful gardens, music, and dancing. Since the gardens were public, the social classes mixed freely.

Anna, the Duchess of Bedford, is credited with inventing the afternoon tea early in the nineteenth century. At the time, most English people had two meals a day, breakfast and dinner. Lady Anna decided she needed a snack before dinner and made a practice of serving tea and a few sweets to guests for a late afternoon pick-me-up. The idea caught on and soon spread across England.

Wealthy tea lovers mourned the growth of tea's popularity among the country's poor. The upper class eventually lobbied Parliament to raise taxes on tea so the less privileged would not be able to afford it.

The Steep Cost of Tea

The taxes imposed on tea stirred up passions in England. At one point, Parliament placed a 119 percent tax on tea—putting it out of reach of the lower classes. Demand did not diminish, though, and it presented an opportunity to entrepreneurs. Tea smugglers went to great—and often violent—lengths to get tea to England ahead of the established East India Company. Soon the tea smuggling trade began to eat into East India Company profits.

Meanwhile, the East India Company's political and economic strength increased in India and China.

Russian Tea Caravans

About the same time England was falling in love with tea, Russia was finding a way to transport the precious leaves across land. The Treaty of Nerchinsk established and opened up a border between Russia and China, allowing tea caravans to transport tea across Mongolia. The trip covered 11,000 miles and took 16 months. Since the most travel-tested animals were camels, long caravans of camels crisscrossed the Russian countryside. These caravans journeying to a mysterious foreign land became the stuff of literature and legend in Russia.

It was given the power to create money, establish governments in the name of Britain, build forts and arm them, and even declare war.

Demand for tea imported from China grew, but England didn't have a lot to offer in trade. The East India Company dealt mostly in silver, but by the early nineteenth century, the demand for tea far outstripped that for silver. To meet the need, the East India Company began illegally growing and trading opium to China in exchange for tea. Despite China's 1799 ban on opium imports, the opium exchange continued into the nineteenth century. China stepped up efforts to curb opium imports, ordering the death penalty for anyone caught bringing the drug into the country. This ignited the first Opium War in 1840, which won Britain the right to trade opium and awarded Hong Kong to Britain. The second war, which ended in 1860, sealed Britain's right to continue trading opium for tea.

Tea Brews Trouble in America

Though the Dutch American colony of New Amsterdam was introduced to tea before England discovered it, the English colonists didn't hear about tea until 1670—about 20 years after England first enjoyed the drink. By 1720, tea was regular cargo on British trade ships headed to America. The colonists, like their British counterparts, turned to smuggling tea to avoid the high taxes imposed on it.

Widespread smuggling cost the East India Company—the only British company allowed to legally import tea—dearly. They lobbied Parliament, which granted the company the exclusive right to ship tea to America duty free, undercutting the smugglers and causing rumbles of rebellion among the colonists. The colonists registered their indignation in one of  the most famous protests of all time: the Boston Tea Party. On December 16, 1773, a group of Bostonians dressed as Native Americans boarded an East India Company ship loaded with 342 crates of tea. They threw every box of tea into Boston Harbor, costing the East India Company about $1 million in today's currency. In response, England closed the port and Parliament passed laws known as the Intolerable Acts that limited the political rights of colonists. These punitive measures helped unite the colonies against British rule. Tea was one of the sparks that ignited the American Revolution.

Race for the Cup

In the nineteenth century, two important events altered the tea-trade landscape. First, China's isolationism and trade limits prompted the East India Company to look to India for tea. Tea was soon growing in Assam and Darjeeling, giving tea lovers new flavors of tea to enjoy. The second event was the repealing of the Navigation Acts in 1849, which finally ended the East India Company's monopoly on Eastern trade.

These new resources combined with a newly freed market led to a flurry of ships racing each other to get to India and China and back to London's tea exchange. A new type of ship, the clipper ship, was designed to speed passage around the world. These light, narrow ships could navigate the waters at record speeds. In parlors and coffeehouses through-out England and America, people would bet on which ship would return in the

fastest time. The new market opened the door for tea to gain popularity around the world.

Another Golden Age for Tea

By the mid-nineteenth century, tea had resumed its place as a staple at English tables. Following Queen Victoria's lead, British citizens elevated tea drinking to an art form. Afternoon tea became an event, and tearooms sprang up across England. At the turn of the twentieth century, tea dances became can't-miss events for Britain's upper and middle classes. During World War II, tea was such a critical staple that it was stocked in 500 places throughout the country to guarantee the supply would remain constant and not be destroyed by German bombing raids.

In America, tea experienced a similar golden age that continues to this day. One hot day at the 1904 St. Louis World's Fair, tea plantation owner Richard Blechyden realized he wasn't going to get any takers for his free samples of hot tea. To avoid wasting his stock, Blechyden iced his tea, and the beverage was a hit. Today,

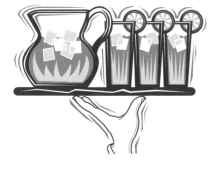

85 percent of the tea consumed in the United States is iced tea, according to the Tea Association of the United States.

In 1908, four years after the creation of iced tea, New York tea merchant Thomas Sullivan inadvertently invented tea bags. As a cost-cutting measure, he wrapped his tea samples in small silk bags to send to prospective customers. He had no idea that they would steep the entire sample, but they thought that's what he had intended. His customers were sorely disappointed when their orders did not arrive packaged in the little silk bags, and they clamored for them. The cost of packaging the tea in silk would have been prohibitive, so Sullivan used gauze instead. His idea certainly caught on: Today, 60 percent of all tea in America is brewed from a tea bag.

All About Tea

Three million tons of tea are produced world-wide each year, and their journey from plantation to teacup combines art and science, ancient tradition and modern innovation.

From One Plant Come Many Cups

There are an estimated 3,000 varieties of tea produced worldwide. With so many different types of tea, you might think there are many different plants that produce them. But that's not the case: All tea leaves trace their roots to one plant. It's the processing the leaves undergo after they are harvested that determines whether they will become black, oolong (wu-long), green, or white tea.

All true tea comes from the leaves of an evergreen shrub, *Camellia sinensis,* a relative of the ornamental camellia plant *(Camellia japonica)* that is grown for its beautiful flowers. There are two main species: One variety, called *Thea sinensis,* is native to China, while the other, *Thea assamica,* hails from India. Other tea plant species are hybrids, made by crossbreeding *Thea sinensis* and *Thea assamica.*

Where in the World Is *Camellia Sinensis*?

Most of the top tea-producing countries are located close to the equator. China, India, Sri Lanka, Japan, and Indonesia grow 85 to 90 percent of the world's tea supply.

While the climate in the United States isn't particularly well suited to commercial tea growing, two states—Hawaii and South Carolina—are home to tea plantations. Black tea is grown on a Wadmalow Island plantation near Charleston, South Carolina. Tea growing in Hawaii began as an experiment in 2000, with the cooperation of the United States Department of Agriculture, to help diversify Hawaii's agricultural economy. Hawaiian tea growers are hoping to develop a specialty niche market for their artisan tea, much like there is for the popular gourmet Kona coffee.

Tea Wannabes

Herbal tea is not really tea because it doesn't come from the *Camellia sinensis* plant. Herbal teas are *tisanes,* or infusions, of herb leaves, roots, seeds, or flowers in hot water. Some true teas, like Earl Grey, are black teas blended with an herb or essential oil. But unless a product contains leaves from the *Camellia sinensis* plant, it is not truly tea.

Getting Picky

Tea is one of the only crops worldwide that is still picked primarily by hand, and the harvesters descend on the plantation when the first leaves begin to peek out from the stem. Harvesting machines can be used to pick tea on level fields, but handpicking is preferred. Good tea is based on the quality of the leaves, and many growers believe that machine picking allows too many older, inferior leaves and stems to accidentally get into the mix, resulting in a lower-quality tea.

It's painstaking work to harvest tea because only the top two youngest leaves on the tip of the stem and the

Seasonal Tastes

Although the tea-grading system can be quite complicated, there is universal agreement when it comes to the season in which the leaf is picked. Leaves picked at "first flush," or first harvest, in the early spring have a lighter taste, while those picked during the "second flush," from late spring through early summer, have a stronger, fuller flavor. Autumnal flushes have their own unique flavor, depending on the region in which they are grown. The flush-number grade is a descriptor, rather than an assigned grade. Which flush one prefers is a matter of individual taste.

unopened leaf bud are picked. Harvesters return every 7 to 10 days during the growing season to remove the youngest leaves.

The Lowdown on Leaves

Tea leaves have a unique combination of constituents, including essential oils, flavonoids, tannins, and caffeine. These, along with climate and growing conditions, influence a tea's flavor. But a particular tea's flavor is also dependent on the way the leaves are processed.

The first step, withering (or wilting), begins immediately after the leaves are harvested. Withering causes leaves to lose one-quarter to one-half their weight and become soft and pliable. Typically, the leaves are spread on large racks and left to dry for 10 to 24 hours. Some growers speed up the process by using large fans to gently circulate the air, some wither in cooler temperatures, while some wither tea leaves in the sun. After withering, the real task of processing begins.

Whether a tea becomes black, green, oolong, or white depends on when the leaves are crushed or broken after withering and how long the leaves are allowed to oxidize, or ferment, before they are dried. The longer the leaves are exposed to air, the more they will ferment. During fermentation the leaves darken because the chlorophyll they contain breaks down, and the tannins are released.

In general, black tea is fully fermented, oolong is partially fermented, green tea is not fermented or only minimally fermented, and white tea is entirely unfermented.

Each tea producer uses its own proprietary process to create its own unique varieties, but there are some general principles used in the making of each type of tea.

Black tea. Black tea takes the most time to make and is the most processed form of tea. First the withered leaves are rolled and bruised (the more traditional method) or cut, torn, and curled (the CTC method) to rupture the cells in the leaves and release some of the essential oils. As these oils come in contact with air, the leaves begin to oxidize (oils and chemicals in the leaf react with the oxygen in the air—the same thing happens when metal rusts or a cut apple turns brown). This process is also known as fermentation. Oxidizing causes the leaves to turn brown and gives a richer flavor and a darker color to the brew.

Black tea leaves are allowed to oxidize for about three to four hours. The leaves are then dried, or fired, by passing them on trays through a hot air chamber. This firing stops the oxidation process and preserves the leaves. The leaves are now dark, or black—which is why this type of tea is called black tea—and are sorted, graded (see Making the Grade, page 24), and readied for packaging.

Oolong tea. Tea leaves destined to become oolong oxidize for a shorter period of time than those for black—only about one to two hours—though growers vary the oxidation time to produce unique flavors. Oolong leaves are typically rolled and sold loose as full leaves rather than cut for tea bags. Oolong is considered the "champagne of tea" and can vary from bright amber to pale yellow in color and from light and floral or fruity to smoky in flavor.

Green tea. Immediately after withering, leaves designated for green tea are heated to prevent oxidation. The Japanese use steam, while the Chinese prefer pan-frying. After heating, the leaves are cooled and rolled into various shapes. These leaves remain green, and they make a pale brew with a very light, sometimes astringent, grassy flavor.

White tea. White tea is made from the unopened leaf buds, which have a white fuzzy undercoat. Some tea companies shield the buds from sunlight while they are growing to prevent chlorophyll from forming. White tea buds are usually not withered. Rather, they are dried immediately after harvesting to prevent any oxidation. White tea requires a lot more individual attention, from picking to processing, than any other tea variety. Though production is increasing, white tea is rare and is usually more expensive than the more common varieties. It brews into an almost colorless liquid with a delicate flavor and aroma.

Making the Grade

Once tea leaves are processed, they are given a grade. They're not like the grades you got in school, though. Tea grades have lots of letters, and they're used to describe the tea in terms of the size and quality of the leaves. There are hundreds of grades, and the grading system is extremely complicated. The categories change depending on the country of origin, the region from which the leaves hail, and even the plantation on which the tea was grown. And there are separate grading methods—and names of grades—for black, green, oolong, and white varieties. Here's a sampling of the most common:

Best of the Black

Black tea makes up 98 percent of the international tea market, so there are many more varieties and grades of black tea. There are four basic sizes of black tea leaves: leaf, broken leaf, fannings (smaller than broken leaf), and dust (the smallest grade, almost a powder). Size does matter, but it isn't the final determination of tea quality. Generally, the smaller the leaf size, the faster the tea brews, giving the final product a darker shade and a more intense

The Mystery of the Orange Pekoe

If you buy your tea from a box in the grocery aisle, chances are you've noticed boxes labeled *orange pekoe*. Of course, one sip will tell you it doesn't taste a bit like orange. Orange pekoe is a very common type of black tea, but the name doesn't describe the flavor; it describes the size of the leaf. Some believe that the Dutch East India Company labeled its tea orange pekoe as an early marketing scheme to connect the tea with the Netherland's royal House of Orange. The word pekoe (pronounced *peck-oh*) may have originated as a Dutch mispronunciation of the Chinese word *bai hao*, which refers to the newest tea leaf buds. Ironically, the tea found in those grocery-shelf boxes of tea is not orange pekoe in the purist sense—because most bagged teas are a blend of many types of teas.

Did you know?

In China, black tea is called red tea because the tea brews up a reddish color, even though the leaves are black.

flavor. The larger, whole leaves offer a smoother flavor and a lighter-colored brew.

Black teas are typically described by the term *pekoe* (pronounced *peck-oh*). Pekoe is accompanied by a long list of adjectives that more specifically classify the tea. Tippy, for instance, is a modifier added to both whole and broken leaf grades to let the buyer know that there are buds in the tea. (The more buds, the higher the quality.) Acronyms are created out of all the terms associated with a particular tea, and the acronym is stamped or printed on the outside of the tea chest or tea box for ready reference. The more letters, the higher quality the tea.

Here's a small sampling of the black tea grades and their accompanying acronyms.

Pekoe (P). Leaves that are shorter and less wiry than orange pekoe—may also be called early pekoe.

Orange pekoe (OP). This describes the unbroken leaf. While orange pekoe is not necessarily a better tea, the leaves are thin and rolled and make an overall good presentation.

Broken orange pekoe fannings (BOPF).
Smallest of tea particles from the tea leaf. What you usually find in your tea bags.

Golden Flowery Orange Pekoe (GFOP). The whole orange pekoe leaf, unrolled, with a golden tip. This tip coloring indicates that the leaf buds were picked when they were young and tender.

Supreme Finest Tippy Golden Flowery Orange Pekoe (FTGFOP). The very highest quality flowery orange pekoe with the most golden tips.

Souchong (S). This is a coarser, flat leaf and is sometimes the fourth leaf of the shoot. Though it is considered to be a lower-quality tea leaf, it has a bold taste. It's grown most often in Taiwan and China.

Oolong Winners

The vast majority of oolong teas are made in Taiwan, and the Taiwanese government developed the grading system for it. Like all tea grading, this one can be a bit complicated. This system is based on the taste of the brew, not on the leaf size or quality. Most oolong grading includes the following categories (plus some subcategories), from lowest to highest grade: Standard, On Good, Good, Fully Good, Good Up, Good to Superior, On Superior, Superior,

Try Chai

Chai (rhymes with *tie,* with the *ch* sound as in *chair*) is a spiced tea and milk drink that is traditional in India. The main ingredients are black tea; milk; a combination of spices that usually includes cinnamon, cardamom, ginger, and pepper; and a sweetener such as honey. Chai is strong and spicy, and it's usually made from a lower grade of tea. In India, chai is sold by street vendors called *chai wallahs.* Chai has become increasingly popular in the United States and is available everywhere from specialty coffeehouses to local groceries. You can buy it freshly made or bottled, as well as powdered to make an instant chai beverage. While it traditionally is served hot, chai can also be made cold or iced.

Fully Superior, Superior Up, Superior to Fine, On Fine, Fine, Fine Up, Fine to Finest, Finest, Finest to Choice.

Grading the Green and White

Each Asian country has its own complex terminology for grading green and white teas. The system involves many categories and subcategories. For Chinese green tea, the grade is based on the age of the leaf before processing and the shape of the leaf after processing. Some Chinese green teas that have varying grades are Gunpowder, Imperial, and Young

Hyson. Japanese green teas are graded by district, style, and cup quality. Some common grading terms used for green and white tea are: Extra Choicest, Choicest, Choice, Finest Fine, Good Medium, Medium, Good Common, Common, Nubs, Dust, and Fannings.

Creating the Perfect Cup

About 90 percent of the tea sold at your local market is a blend of many teas. Blending allows manufacturers to provide a consistent flavor for their brand and keeps the price stable, despite the weather or market factors. To create the taste that a customer has come to rely on, a manufacturer will blend together dozens of different teas. Some even use 70 different teas to get just the right flavor.

Tea manufacturers typically send specialized buyers to hundreds of tea estates to sample their teas and select those that will best suit their blends. Once the teas arrive at the blending factory, they are combined and tested by highly trained tea tasters who have spent years learning to detect the variations of texture, taste, and aroma of brewed teas.

Winning the Tea Title

Like winemakers, tea growers take great pride in the subtle differences of flavor and character in their tea. To showcase their products, many tea growers take their tea to competition each year. The World Tea Competition, one of the largest, is held each summer and typically ends with the winner auctioning their tea to major tea suppliers. Winning the World Tea Competition can really boost the reputation and the income of the winning tea grower. In 2006, the World Tea Competition took place in Taiwan and included more than 750 tea growers from 15 Asian countries.

Tea blending is an art, and it requires a sensitive palate and a keen nose. On any given day, a tea taster may sample 200 to 1,000 cups of tea. Just like wine tasters, tea tasters first sniff the brew. Then they sip a bit, swish it around in their mouths, and spit it out. The tasters determine which teas and what amounts of them will exactly match the control version of a particular tea.

Many tea manufacturers add other flavorings or scents to their teas. These can be added during the processing stage at the tea plantation, or they can be added at the blending factory. Jasmine tea, for instance, is made by spreading jasmine flowers into the tea while it is oxidizing, while spices such as cinnamon or flavorings such as lemon are commonly added at the factory.

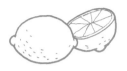

A Buffet of Brews

With an estimated 3,000 types of teas, it's easy to feel a bit overwhelmed. Here's a primer on some of the most popular types of traditional tea.

Tea	Type of Tea Leaf	Taste
Assam	Black	strong, rich flavor
Darjeeling	Black	lighter flavor, sweet
Earl Grey	Black	fragrant, infused with oil of bergamot
English Breakfast	Black	bold, rich flavor, good with milk
Lapsang Souchong	Black	smoky, bold flavor
Jasmine	Oolong	fragrant, light flavor
Oolong	Oolong	fragrant, mild flavor
Gunpowder	Green	light, delicate flavor
Silver Needle	White	extremely mild, almost flavorless

Tea and Your Health

*Could good health be brewing in your cup of tea?
Some research suggests so. Tea may help prevent
diseases such as cardiovascular disease (or heart
disease), cancer, diabetes, and osteoporosis.*

Tea's Triple Power

Before tea became a beloved and much sought-after
beverage worldwide, it was used medicinally. The
Chinese credited it as a remedy for everything from
headaches to melancholy. In recent years we've
come full circle, and tea is once again being touted
for its healing properties. Today we know what
the ancient world did not: Tea has three active
ingredients that contribute to its healing power—
flavonoids, fluoride, and caffeine. But the flavonoids
are responsible for most of tea's health benefits.

Go Green—with Flavonoids

Research has shown an indisputable link between
eating plant foods and good health. Vegetables
and fruits contain an array of vitamins, minerals,

and phytochemicals, plant compounds that have health-protective and disease-preventive properties. Tea, which comes from the *Camellia sinensis* plant, also has an abundance of phytochemicals.

There are thousands of phytochemicals in plants. Tea leaves contain a subgroup called polyphenols, or tea polyphenols, that include flavonoids. Polyphenols—including flavonoids—are powerful antioxidants, which are critical to your health because they act as a kind of defense system for your body. Antioxidants help neutralize destructive forms of oxygen or nitrogen known as free radicals, which are unstable molecules that steal electrons from the molecules of healthy cells. Antioxidents protect cells by binding to free radicals and neutralizing them before they can damage DNA or other cell components. In addition to their antioxidant activity, flavonoids can also help regulate how cells function.

> Better to be deprived of food for three days than tea for one.
>
> —*Chinese Proverb*

Tea is particularly high in flavonoids, higher than many vegetables or fruits. Tea provides about 83 percent of the total intake of flavonoids in the

American adult diet, followed by citrus fruit juices (4 percent), and wine (2 percent), according to a 2007 study in the *American Journal of Nutrition*.

Among the foods and beverages tested, black tea provides the largest number of flavonols—a type of flavonoid—in the U.S. diet (32 percent), according to scientists in the Nutrient Data Laboratory at the USDA Agricultural Research Service.

Flavonoid Levels in Tea— The Ups and Downs

There are thousands of flavonoids, but one type called catechins is currently in the limelight. Of special interest is epigallocatechin gallate (EGCG), a compound that is thought to be an especially powerful antioxidant. Researchers believe EGCG may be a key to the development of new drugs or complementary therapies to treat disease. Other tea catechins called epicatechin (EC), epigallocatechin (EGC), and epicatechin gallate (ECG) are also being investigated.

Green and white tea have an abundance of EGCG— more than black or oolong, both of which contain many other types of antioxidants that scientists have studied for their healing benefits. In fact, a cup of green tea has more catechins than an apple, according to the USDA Database for the Flavonoid Content of Selected Foods, 2007.

Different kinds of tea have different kinds of flavonoids. That's important because different flavonoids appear to play different roles in protecting the body from disease. While green tea has the most EGCG, black and oolong teas have more of the complex flavonoids called thearubigins and teaflavins. These are formed during the fermentation process and have been found to offer protection against heart attacks and cardiovascular disease.

Black, green, and oolong teas are a good source of the flavonols kaempferol, quercetin, and myricetin,

Daily Dose

Studies of green tea have tested the effects of drinking between 1 and 10 cups per day (containing 8 ounces each), with most studies using 4 cups per day as a possible therapeutic dose. This amounts to about 750 milligrams (mg) of EGCG, the most powerful antioxidant found in green tea. Brewed green tea has 188 mg of EGCG per cup, while black tea has 22 mg. You can buy green tea as an extract in pill form, but these products are not standardized, so they vary in strength. Currently there is no recommended daily dose.

which help relax blood vessels, improve blood flow, and reduce inflammation in cells, among other benefits.

Fluoride

The tea plant absorbs fluoride from the soil and from fertilizers, and the mineral accumulates in the leaves over time. The amount of fluoride in brewed tea varies depending on the type of leaf, the brewing time, and the amount of fluoride in the water. In general, higher quality tea, which is made from younger leaves, contains less fluoride. That means white tea, which is made from the very youngest, unopened leaf buds, is unlikely to have much fluoride at all. Of the more common teas, oolong tea has the least fluoride (0.1–0.2 mg per 8 ounces) while black tea has the most (0.2–0.5 mg per 8 ounces). Green tea is in between the two with 0.3–0.4 mg per 8 ounces. Brick tea, a lower grade of tea made from older leaves and stems, has the most fluoride of all (0.5–1.7 mg per 8 ounces), but it is rarely consumed in the United States. The flouride content provided above does not include the water in which the tea is brewed.

In adequate doses, fluoride strengthens both teeth and bones, protecting against cavities and bone-density loss. The U.S. Institute of Medicine recommends that adults get 3 to 4 mg of fluoride per day, and that children get 0.7 to 2 mg per day, depending on their age and body weight.

A recent Japanese study found that rinsing the mouth with green tea prevented the production of acid as well as the growth of bacteria that cause cavities. And a small study in Italy found that drinking black tea helped prevent cavities and plaque.

Too much fluoride, however, can cause fluorosis, a condition in which the teeth become mottled and discolored. In severe cases, the tooth enamel becomes soft and crumbly. Excess fluoride intake can also cause brittle bones.

Caffeine

Caffeine is a stimulant that increases heart rate, makes you alert, and revs up metabolism. All *Camellia sinensis* teas naturally contain caffeine, but the amount varies depending on the grade and type of tea, whether it is brewed from loose leaves or a tea bag, and how long it is brewed.

Black tea has the most caffeine (42 to 72 mg per 8 ounces) while green, white, and oolong teas have less (9 to 50 mg per 8 ounces). Compare those amounts with the caffeine content of coffee, which has 110 to 140 mg per 8 ounces. Decaffeinated teas only have 1 to 4 mg per 8 ounces.

Being Careful with Caffeine. While caffeine provides health benefits, it can cause problems when it interacts with certain medications. Caffeine is known to both enhance and interfere with certain drugs. For example, taking the antibiotic ciprofloxacin (Cipro) with caffeine can increase nervousness, anxiety, and heart pounding.

Time and Temperature

One 2006 study in Taiwan found that the hotter the water, the faster the tea leaves would release antioxidants and caffeine into the brew. Steeping in cold water takes longer to produce a brew with the same level of antioxidants and caffeine.

Caffeine may interact with epinephrine, a drug used to treat severe allergic reactions and acute asthma attacks that don't respond to other asthma medication, causing dangerously high blood pressure.

Because caffeine is a diuretic, it will increase the effects of diuretic drugs, which are often prescribed for high blood pressure. And caffeine may interfere with the action of antianxiety or muscle-relaxant medications such as Valium and Ativan, and other psychoactive drugs, especially MAO inhibitors.

Caffeine can increase the stomach's production of acid and can exacerbate the symptoms of acid reflux or ulcers.

A Healing Cup—Tea and Disease

Research over the last decade has begun to prove what the ancients divined: Tea does have properties that can help prevent or lower the risk of certain diseases. It's the constituents in tea that we discussed at the beginning of the chapter, particularly the flavonoids and other polyphenols, that give tea its healing power. All types of tea—black, green, oolong, and white—as well as tea extracts, have been studied, and each has its own particular disease-fighting and disease-preventing constituents.

Evidence supporting the health benefits of tea consumption continues to mount, but the following is what research shows thus far to be tea's contributions to good health.

Heart Disease—Tea and Your Ticker

Heart disease is the leading cause of death in the United States, but tea drinking may be able to shrink that number. Some research shows that black and green tea both help fight the development of cardiovascular diseases including heart attack and stroke. A number of studies have shown that tea consumption can slow down the progression of atherosclerosis, or hardening of the arteries. Tea has also been shown to lower LDL, or "bad," cholesterol and relax blood vessels, which can lower blood pressure. These are all important steps in preventing heart disease.

A 2002 University of North Carolina statistical review of many different tea studies found that people who drink three or more cups of black tea each day have a moderately reduced risk (about 11 percent) of heart disease and stroke compared to those who do not drink tea.

 The results of a Saudi national study, published in 2003, show a significantly lower incidence of heart disease among those who drank more than six cups of black tea per day compared to those

who did not, even after adjusting for other risk factors such as smoking and age. The study compared tea consumption and the incidence of coronary heart disease in 3,430 Saudi Arabian men and women between the ages of 30 and 70. Those who drank black tea were found to have lower cholesterol and triglyceride levels as well.

Green tea seems to offer cardiovascular protection, too. An 11-year study that followed the tea consumption of more than 40,000 people in Japan found that people who drank more than five cups of green tea a day were 26 percent less likely to die of cardiovascular disease during the study period and 16 percent less likely to die from any cause at all. The study was published in the September 13, 2006, issue of *The Journal of the American Medical Association.*

Another large study of overall diet in Japan published in 2007 found that people who drank green tea in addition to eating a traditional Japanese diet of fruits, vegetables, soy, and seaweed had a significantly lower incidence of cardiovascular disease than those whose diets were higher in red meat and dairy and lower in tea. This was evident despite the the healthier group's tendency to consume more sodium and to have high blood pressure.

Cancer

All kinds of tea have been studied for their effects against various cancers, both in laboratory and human studies, with mixed results. Scientists caution that it's too soon to tell for sure if tea will help battle cancer.

The best results have been seen in the laboratory. EGCG, the powerful antioxidant most abundant in green tea, inhibits cancer in a number of ways in lab experiments. It binds to free radicals and neutralizes them before they can damage healthy cells. It also seems to slow, and even reduce, the size of tumors in some animal models.

There's also evidence that EGCG reduces the growth of new blood cells that would feed tumors,

An Inconvenient Tea Truth

To get the maximum number of antioxidants from tea, you have to brew it yourself. According to the U.S. Department of Agriculture, instant teas and bottled teas contain very few antioxidants. Manufacturers are not required to put this information on their labels. The good news? You can use the convenient tea bag to brew your own and still get plenty of antioxidants.

at least in lab experiments. And it seems that EGCG can inhibit the production of COX-2, an enzyme produced by tumors that causes inflammation and can lead to further tumor growth.

Laboratory studies are a first step, but the findings aren't always replicated in human studies. Studies of people who drink green, black, or oolong tea don't always show a clear-cut benefit. Some studies show a protective effect against certain cancers, while others do not.

The differences in these studies may be explained by the variations in overall diet, environment, and genetics among the study groups. And since no two pots of tea are exactly the same, the participants aren't taking in a standardized number of flavonoids. Many human studies are based on surveys that ask participants to recall what they ate and drank, how often, and how much. These can be quite unreliable, leading to false study conclusions.

The type of cancer is also a significant factor in determining tea's protective and healing benefits. Some cancers appear to be more greatly impacted by tea than others. Here's a rundown of the types of cancer that have been studied:

Skin Cancer and Radiation Damage. Green tea appears to offer some protection against skin cancer. Whether taken as a drink or applied to the skin, the antioxidants in green tea seem to protect against cell damage, tumor growth, and even some of the effects of aging. The studies that have been done are mostly on mice or small groups of people, and scientists don't yet understand exactly how green tea protects skin from the sun.

A study in the December 2006 issue of the *British Medical Journal* reported that green tea extract could help people with skin damage from radiation treatments. Cancer patients undergoing radiation applied preparations of either black or green tea extracts to their radiation sites for ten minutes a day. After 16 days, the patients using green tea extract saw some skin improvement; those using black tea extract saw improvement after 22 days. In addition to working more quickly, the green tea extract was more effective. Researchers concluded the polyphenols in green tea are beneficial to skin, although they said other compounds may be at work as well.

Warning: Green tea is NOT a sunscreen. Cosmetic companies have rushed to include green tea extract in many skin care products, and while they may help prevent skin cancer, this effect hasn't been well studied in humans, and they absolutely should NOT take the place of tried-and-true sunscreens.

Prostate Cancer. Prostate cancer research has focused on the effects of green tea with some success, especially in the area of inhibiting the enzyme COX-2. A 2007 laboratory experiment at the University of Wisconsin, Madison, determined that EGCG, when combined with a COX-2 inhibitor drug, was more effective at inhibiting cancer cells than just the drug alone. The results were seen in both a laboratory strain of human prostate cancer cells and in mice with prostate cancer.

In a 2006 Italian study published in *Cancer Research,* 60 volunteers with premalignant lesions who were at risk of developing prostate cancer were given capsules of green tea powder or a placebo daily for one year. Only 3 percent of the subjects given the green tea developed prostate cancer compared to 30 percent of the subjects given the placebo. This suggests that green tea may help prevent or delay the progression of this disease.

Breast Cancer. In cell culture and animal experiments, green tea has been shown to stop breast cancer cells from growing. Studies showing an effect of green tea on breast cancer in humans are few but, in general, they have shown some benefit, particularly on cancer recurrence among women who had early stage breast cancer.

In a 2003 study of 1,095 Asian-American women in Los Angeles County, green tea drinkers were shown to have a significantly lower risk of developing breast cancer. Compared to women who drank no tea at all, the risk of breast cancer was 47 percent lower among those who drank green tea daily. This effect was even more pronounced in women with low levels of an enzyme known to eliminate polyphenols rapidly from the body.

Lung Cancer. A 2001 study of 1,324 women living in Shanghai, China, showed that drinking green tea reduced the risk of developing lung cancer by 35 percent among those who were nonsmokers.

Although a cigarette smoker's risk of lung cancer is about 20 times higher than that of someone who has never smoked, drinking tea may offer a small amount of protection, according to several studies.

Researchers stress that most of the studies investigating the impact of green tea on lung cancer have been small, and no one is suggesting that tea can cancel the damaging effects of cigarette smoke. At best, green tea may ameliorate some of the deleterious effects of smoking. Smoking is still the largest preventable cause of lung cancer, and diet alone is not enough to overcome the ill effects it has on the body.

Tea for Diabetes Control

Observational studies conducted in large populations have shown that people who consume green tea have a lower risk of developing type 2 diabetes, the most common form of diabetes among adults. A couple of smaller studies suggest that black and oolong teas may be preventive as well.

But to date the findings from intervention studies in humans are mixed. One 2005 study in Japan followed 66 patients with diabetes or borderline diabetes who took either 500 mg of powdered green tea polyphenols daily or no green tea pills for two months. They found no clear effect of green tea polyphenols on blood glucose levels or on insulin resistance.

But a 2003 study of Taiwanese adults with diabetes found that drinking oolong tea combined with taking hypoglycemic drugs may be an effective treatment for type 2 diabetes. The participants were on blood glucose-lowering medications and were given either six cups of oolong tea or water per day. After one month, the glucose levels of those given the oolong tea were significantly reduced compared to those given water alone.

Immune System

Green tea may help prevent rheumatoid arthritis or other immune system disorders. Researchers have been prompted to look at green tea's potential because the incidence of these health problems is significantly lower in China and Japan, the two leading consumers of green tea.

In 2003, scientists at Case Western Reserve University treated cartilage tissue cultures with green tea extract and found that the treated cells released less of the enzyme associated with arthritis, joint inflammation, and cartilage deterioration than cells that were not treated with the extract. Doctors already recommend a diet rich in fruits, vegetables, and fish for arthritis patients because antioxidants and omega-3 fatty acids can reduce the symptoms of arthritis. It's likely that green tea offers at least some of the healthful benefits of these foods.

Tea may also boost the body's power to fight bacterial infections. A small study at Brigham and Women's Hospital in 2003 found that patients who drank 20 ounces of black tea per day for two weeks had stronger resistance to infections than did a similar group of coffee drinkers. In fact, the immune system's output of an infection-fighting substance called interferon gamma was doubled or tripled. Researchers noted that the amino acid responsible for the effect, L-theanine, is also present in green and oolong teas.

Bone Density

Although excessive caffeine consumption has been linked with bone loss, preliminary research suggests that drinking any kind of tea may positively impact bone density, despite the caffeine.

Nutritional Value of Tea

Tea is a low-calorie beverage, especially when brewed at home using little or no sugar. A cup of brewed tea without sugar has only 2 calories and no fat, cholesterol, or sodium. It also provides about 12 mcg of folate; 50 mg of potassium; and trace amounts of manganese, magnesium, phosphorous, and other minerals. Adding a small amount of nonfat milk to your tea will increase the calcium content without adding fat.

In 2000, a British study of 1,256 postmenopausal women found that those who were frequent tea drinkers (most often it was black tea) had significantly better bone density than those who didn't drink tea. This finding was replicated in a study published in 2003 by University of Arizona researchers, who examined the bone density and beverage choices of more than 91,000 postmenopausal American women over a four-year period. They found that habitual tea drinkers had greater bone density than did nontea drinkers. However, researchers noted that the tea drinkers were not any less likely to have fractures of the hip, wrist, or forearm.

Green tea also seems to improve bone density, although perhaps in a different way than black tea. Researchers in Taiwan published a study in the *Archives of Internal Medicine* in 2002 suggesting that it's the length of time spent drinking green tea, and not the amount of tea, that increases bone density. More than 1,000 study participants were questioned about their tea drinking habits. About half were habitual tea drinkers, with oolong and green tea consumed most often. Those who had been habitual tea drinkers for six to ten years had greater bone density than those who were not habitual tea drinkers or had been drinking tea for less than six years. There were too few black tea drinkers to determine whether it had the same effect on bone density as green tea. The researchers attributed the effect to fluoride and flavonoids in tea.

What does this mean for you? Tea is a healthy drink, and it may help protect your bones. But drinking it doesn't decrease the necessity of getting enough dietary calcium or of taking prescribed bone-building medication to treat osteoporosis.

Minding Your Memory

In ancient China, green tea was thought to provide mental clarity, and now evidence of that is turning up in laboratory studies.

Experiments on mice and rat brain cells show that green tea antioxidants seem to prevent the formation of an Alzheimer's-related protein, beta-amyloid, which accumulates in the brain as plaque and leads to memory loss. This finding has been  duplicated in a number of other cell-culture experiments. In one of these types of studies the antioxidants in black tea also were protective, although not as much as those in green tea.

In humans, green tea has been associated with a lower risk of dementia and memory loss. A Japanese study published in 2006 in the *American Journal of Clinical Nutrition* surveyed more than 1,000 people older than age 70. Those who drank two or more cups a day of green tea were half as likely to develop dementia and memory loss as those who drank fewer than two cups per week. This effect was much weaker for black and oolong teas.

Kidney Stones

Drinking tea every day may cut your risk of developing kidney stones. In 1998 the Nurses' Health Study, one of the largest investigations into the risk factors for chronic diseases in women, showed an 8 percent decrease in the risk of kidney stones for each 8-ounce cup of tea the women drank daily. (The type of tea was not identified, but the researchers assumed the majority was black tea.)

A Harvard study of 45,389 men in 1996 reported an even greater benefit. For every 8 ounces of tea the men drank daily, they experienced a 14 percent decrease in kidney stone development.

Slimming Down with Tea

Ads touting green tea's ability to help you lose weight may be more than hype. A growing body of research suggests a possible benefit, not just for green tea but for oolong as well.

A study reported in the journal *Obesity* in 2007 found that 31 healthy, lean young participants who drank a mixture of green tea catechins,

A Diet Drink?

Tea may or may not count as a "diet" drink, depending on what else is added to your cup. A cup of plain brewed tea has only about 2 calories, while a 20-ounce whole-milk chai latte at your local beverage shop may pack on more than 300 calories, depending on the brand and kind of sweetener used.

calcium, and caffeine for three days burned 4.6 percent more calories than when they drank plain water. Although this wasn't a huge increase in metabolism, the researchers said it could be enough to help someone succeed at controlling their weight, especially in combination with a healthy diet and exercise. The effects in older, more overweight people have not been demonstrated.

The ancient Chinese believed oolong tea helped control body weight, and at least one modern

Milk and Sugar?

Some studies have explored whether adding milk, sugar, or lemon will dilute tea's healthful effects. There is little published research on the subject, and it offers conflicting opinions. Bottom line? If you like milk or sugar, go ahead and use it in moderation—especially if it means you'll drink more of this healthful beverage. Remember, milk and sugar have calories, and the more you use in your tea, the higher the calorie content will be. Stay away from cream or half-and-half. Low-fat or fat-free milk is the best choice.

study suggests this, too. In 2001, researchers at the USDA Agricultural Research Service gave 12 male volunteers four separate oolong tea formulas (full-strength tea, colored water with the equivalent amount of caffeine to full-strength tea, half-strength tea, and plain colored water) for three days in a row. They measured the men's energy expenditure before and after the experiment and found that the participants burned, on average, 67 more calories per day when they drank tea instead of water. Even more significant to the researchers was that fat oxidation was significantly higher (12 percent) after the full-strength-tea consumption than after the plain-water consumption. The beverage containing water plus caffeine also increased energy expenditure and fat oxidation compared to water alone. It is not clear, then, whether the effects of the tea were due solely to its caffeine content. The researchers tentatively concluded that a component other than caffeine played a role.

Despite these positive studies, others show little or no effect of tea on weight loss. Green tea is a healthy drink, and evidence suggests it might help you burn a few calories, but exercise and a healthful diet are still the best way to slim down.

Tea Is Not for Everyone

If you are anemic or have an iron deficiency, drinking tea within an hour or two of eating foods containing iron may make these conditions worse. The pigments in tea and coffee, called tannins, bind to the iron and interfere with its absorption.

People who are allergic to caffeine or tannins should also avoid tea, as it can cause skin rashes and hives. In fact, there have been a handful of studies documenting severe allergies to green tea, especially among people who work in the tea processing industry.

People who take certain blood-thinning drugs, also called anticoagulants, such as warfarin (Coumadin), need to be cautious about drinking too much green tea. Green tea contains vitamin K, which affects blood clotting. It is not necessary for people on these drugs to avoid green tea entirely. However, large quantities of green tea (eight cups per day or more) may decrease their effectiveness.

People taking anticoagulants should also avoid taking high doses of dietary supplements containing green tea leaves in their powdered form, unless approved by their doctor. Green tea leaves contain a lot of vitamin K; in fact, they have more than five times the amount found in black tea leaves.

Research into the possible health effects of tea is ongoing and will continue to interest researchers in the years to come. Hidden within tea's leaves there may be clues that could lead to new treatments or even cures for diseases in the future. In the meantime, enjoy tea for the simple joy of its taste and aroma and know that in doing so, you may be protecting your health as well.

Making the Perfect Cuppa

Tea connoisseurs may argue about how to produce the perfect cup, but there are just a few simple rules for storing and preparing tea.

Loose Versus Bagged

The path to a great cup of tea begins with the kind of tea you select. Next, you'll have to choose between loose leaf or bagged tea. Each has distinct advantages and disadvantages.

Loose Tea

High-quality teas are almost always sold loose and by the pound. Regardless of the quality, though, there is more selection in loose teas than in bagged ones. A quick online search will reveal thousands of varieties from which to choose, but you can find an ample selection in a tea shop or health food store.

Loose leaves usually produce a more flavorful brew than bagged tea does. That's because they have more contact with the water and more room to expand and infuse their flavor.

Though loose tea is reputed to be more expensive than bagged tea, the opposite is more often the case. Tea bags are usually more expensive because you're paying for convenience.

Tea Bags

Tea bags offer tremendous convenience, and 96 percent of the tea in the United States is sold that way. There are more varieties of tea available in bags today than ever before. You can even find whole-leaf tea in bags (it comes in larger bags, so the leaves have room to expand). Tea made from bags with this type of packaging can equal the quality of loose tea, but it will cost you more per cup.

Critics of tea bags say they contain inferior types of tea. Tea bags most often contain fannings or dust, the two lowest grades of tea. Fannings are small pieces of leaves, while dust is exactly what it sounds like—the tiny particles of leaves left at the bottom of the barrel. Because these small pieces of leaves or dust come into immediate contact with the water, they brew quickly, even instantly. While some find that advantageous, others feel that these teas just color the water and give a bitter taste.

Perhaps the greatest problem with tea bags is that they don't keep fresh for long. More of the tea's surface area is exposed to air because the particles are so small, and the tea goes stale quickly. If you're buying bagged tea, look for those that are individually wrapped so they'll keep fresh longer.

Brewing the Best

How your cup of tea tastes is affected by the quality of the leaves and the amount you use, the freshness and temperature of the water, and the brewing method and steeping time. Once you learn the ropes, you'll be able to produce a perfect cup of tea every time.

Proportions

How much tea you use depends on whether the tea is loose or bagged and how many servings you're making.

Loose tea. The general rule of thumb is to use one heaping teaspoon of tea for each 8-ounce cup of water. Some say you should add "one for the pot," but that's not a hard-and-fast rule. Tea with large leaves or flowers may require more leaves to get a strong enough brew.

Bagged tea. Use one small bag per 8 ounces of water. Don't skimp by using fewer bags and letting them steep longer; this will only create a bitter brew.

H₂O

It may just be plain water, but its purity and temperature are critical to the palatability of your brew.

Water quality. Water for tea should be cold, clear, pure, and well aerated. For the best flavor, brew tea in water that has a high oxygen content—either fresh tap water that's been allowed to run for a while or bottled spring water. Don't reboil, as most of the oxygen will be depleted, and your tea will taste flat. Don't run hot water from the tap to save time; it picks up various tastes from the pipes and will affect the flavor. Chlorine can affect the taste of your tea, too, so consider using a water filter if your tap water is heavily chlorinated.

Water temperature. To brew black or oolong tea, use water that has just reached a rolling boil. Don't let the water continue to boil, as the oxygen will escape. For green tea and white teas, which are more delicate, use water that's just below the boiling point, about 180 degrees Fahrenheit. Boiling water will scald green or white tea, and the brew will taste bitter. Try using a thermometer to get the temperature just right. To prevent overboiling, don't use the microwave. Leave the lid off the teapot while brewing green, white, or oolong tea so it doesn't get too hot.

The Art of Brewing

There's more to brewing tea than a couple quick dunks of a tea bag in hot water!

Brewing method. Swirl some hot water around your mug or teapot, then pour it out before you add the tea and hot water. The bit of steam that results will help soften the tea leaves so they release their flavor more readily. And warming the pot in advance will keep your tea hot longer.

Brewing time. It really does matter, so use a timer or watch for precision. For black varieties, steep three to five minutes. For green or oolong tea, steep only about two minutes. The longer the tea brews, the more bitter it will become.

Brewing equipment. If you use loose leaves, you'll need to remove them when they're finished steeping. This is critical because leaves left in the pot will

Reading Bubbles

If you don't have a thermometer, you can tell how hot the water is by the size of the bubbles. If you see tiny little bubbles clinging to the sides of the pot, the water is about 186°F. Small chains of bubbles that rise from the bottom to the top of the water surface mean the water is 190°F. Rolling bubbles mean the water is boiling, 212°F. If you live at a high altitude, however, this bubble test is not accurate.

eventually make the tea bitter. There are several approaches to brewing and removing leaves:

- Let them float free. The best flavor is achieved when the leaves swirl in the water. Simply hold a wire strainer over the cup or pot to strain out the leaves as you pour. This works well if you're serving the whole pot at once. If you're not, steep the tea in one pot, then pour it into another through a mesh strainer. Keep the second pot warm or strain the tea into an insulated thermos.

- Use a tea ball. These are made of aluminum or mesh and have small holes that allow the water to seep in. Unfortunately, there is rarely enough room for the tea leaves to expand, unfold, and steep properly, especially if you're using enough leaves to brew a whole pot.

- Tea filter inserts. These fit inside the teapot opening. Some teapots come with a filter insert. They're usually big enough to allow the leaves to circulate and are easy to clean.

- Paper filter. These are individual square paper pouches that can be filled with your own loose tea. They come with an adhesive or tuckable flap to keep the tea inside. There are also larger filters for brewing a whole pot.

- Tea press. You stir the leaves into the pot, allow them to brew, then use the plunger to press them down to the bottom. If you don't serve the whole pot at once, however, the leaves will continue to infuse somewhat. And you'll have to clean the leaves out of the bottom of the pot.

Storing Tea

Tea is vulnerable to heat, light, air, and moisture. If any of those come in contact with it, the tea will lose its flavor and aroma and quickly turn stale. Unless it comes in an airtight tin, transfer loose tea to an airtight canister immediately after buying it.

Tea bags that come individually wrapped can be kept in any dry, cool cabinet. But if you buy tea bags that are unwrapped inside a cardboard box, put the tea bags in an airtight canister and throw the box away. Keep it away from the stove and sink to avoid heat and water.

When stored properly, green and white tea leaves are good for about six months to one year, and the darker teas, oolong and black, are good for about one to two years.